MANDOLIN
MANUSCRIPT BOOK

1 2 3 4 5 6 7 8 9 0

Visit us on the Web at www.melbay.com — E-mail us at email@melbay.com

MEL BAY PUBLICATIONS, INC., PACIFIC, MO 63069.

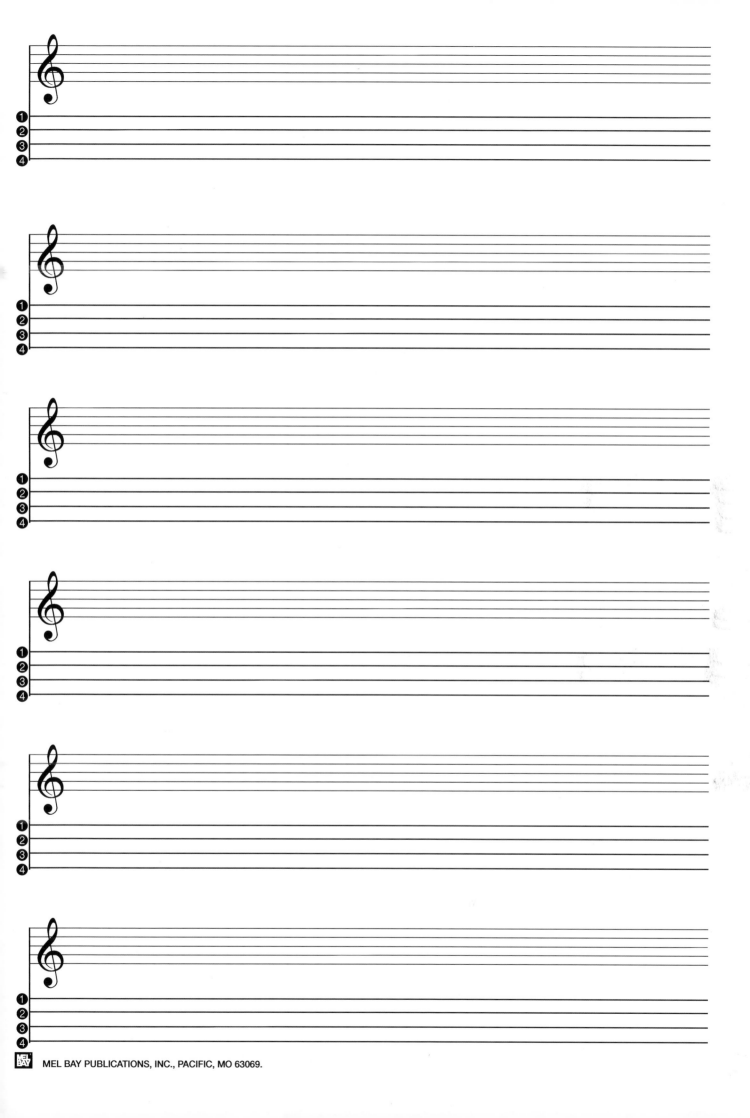

MEL BAY PUBLICATIONS, INC., PACIFIC, MO 63069.

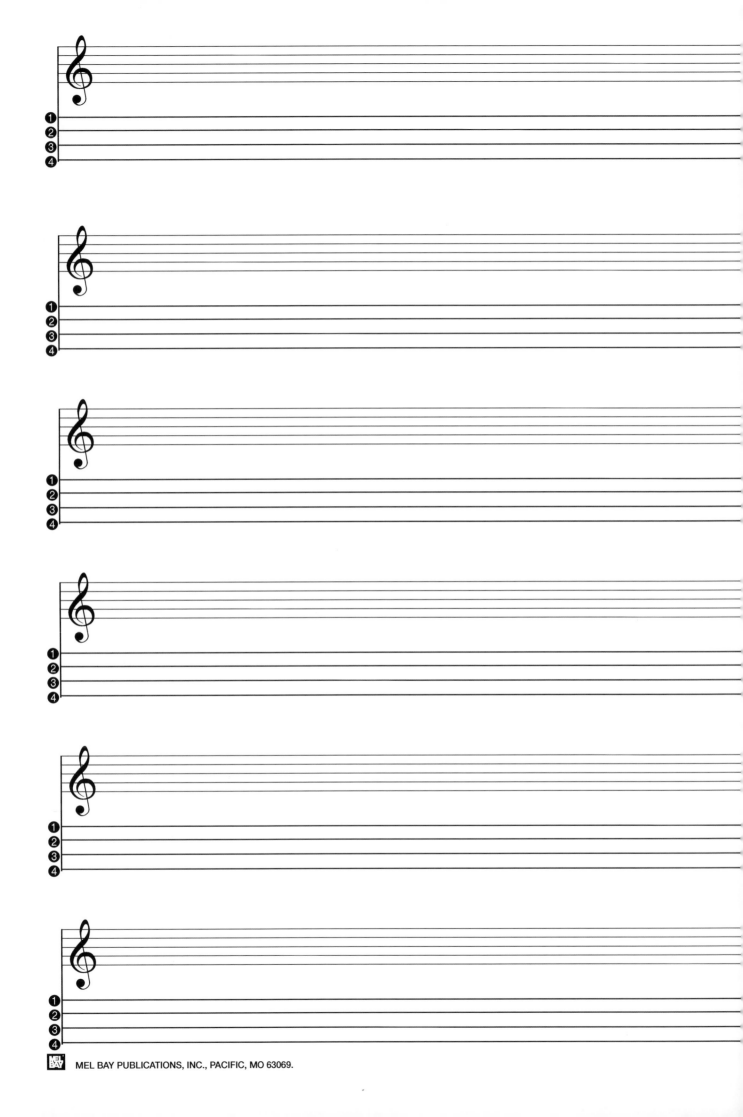

MEL BAY PUBLICATIONS, INC., PACIFIC, MO 63069.

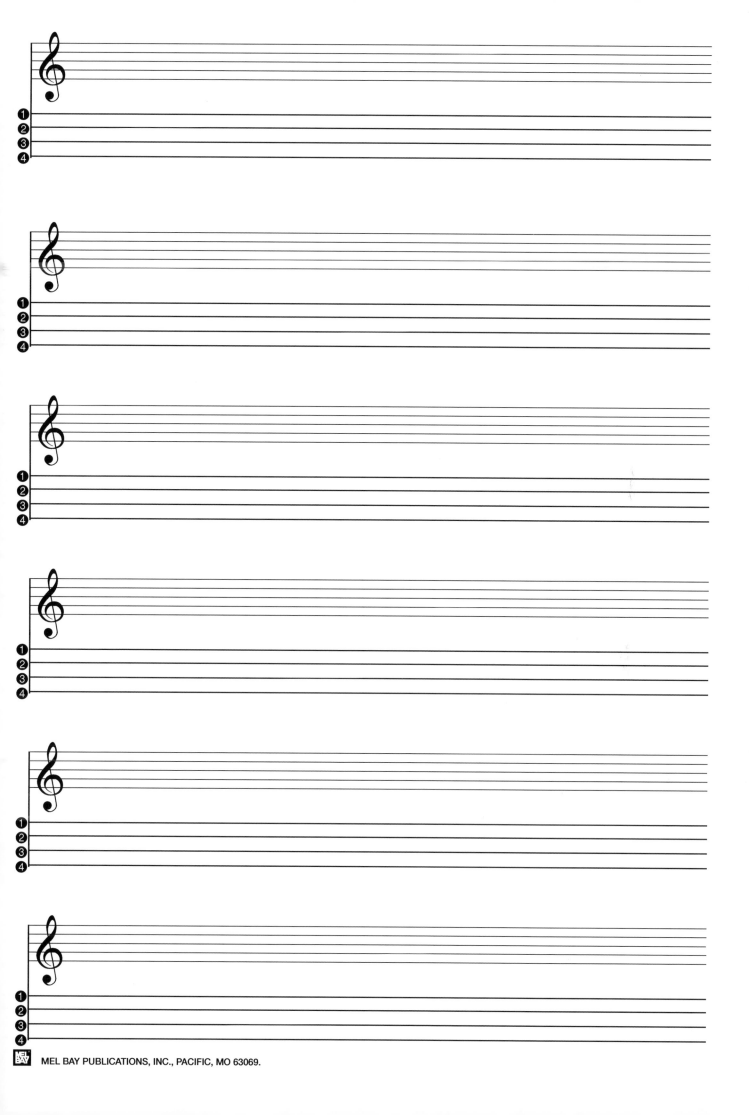

MEL BAY PUBLICATIONS, INC., PACIFIC, MO 63069.

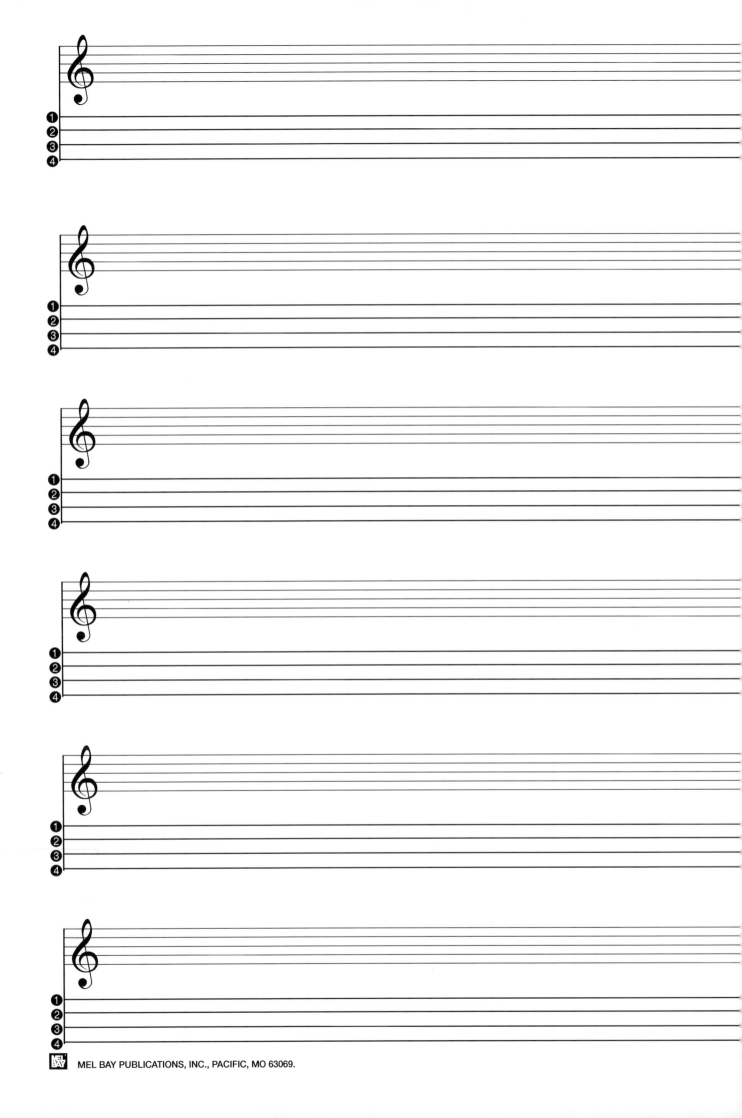

MEL BAY PUBLICATIONS, INC., PACIFIC, MO 63069.

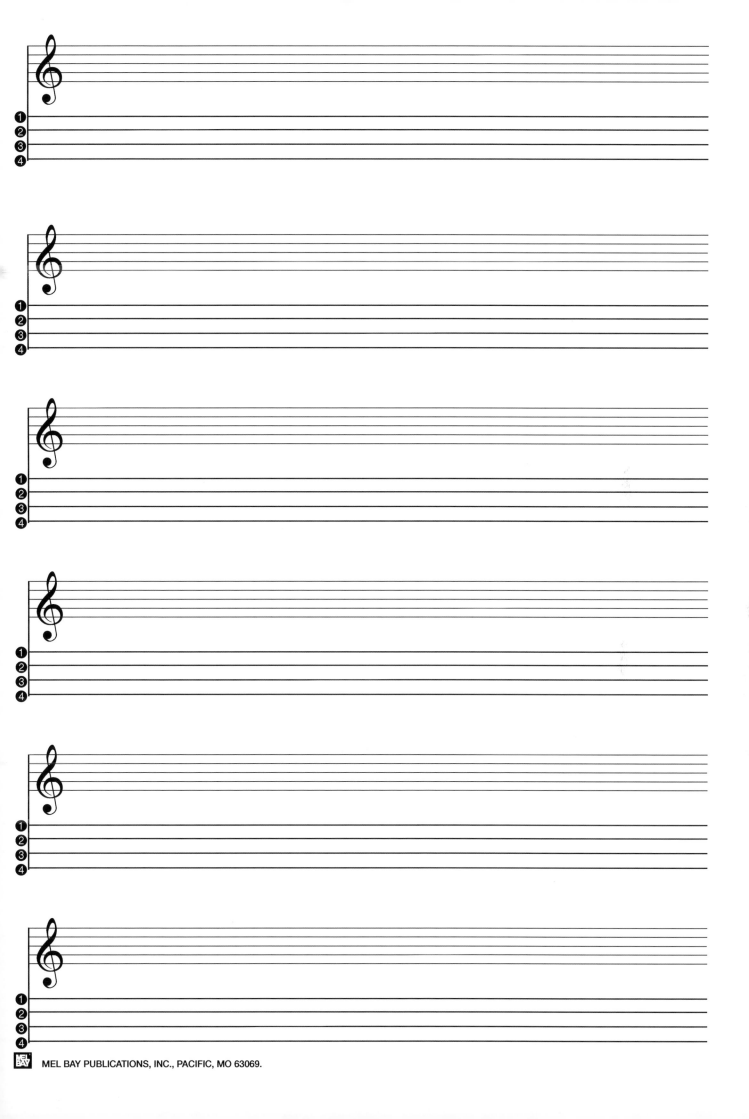

MEL BAY PUBLICATIONS, INC., PACIFIC, MO 63069.

MEL BAY PUBLICATIONS, INC., PACIFIC, MO 63069.

MEL BAY PUBLICATIONS, INC., PACIFIC, MO 63069.

MEL BAY PUBLICATIONS, INC., PACIFIC, MO 63069.

MEL BAY PUBLICATIONS, INC., PACIFIC, MO 63069.

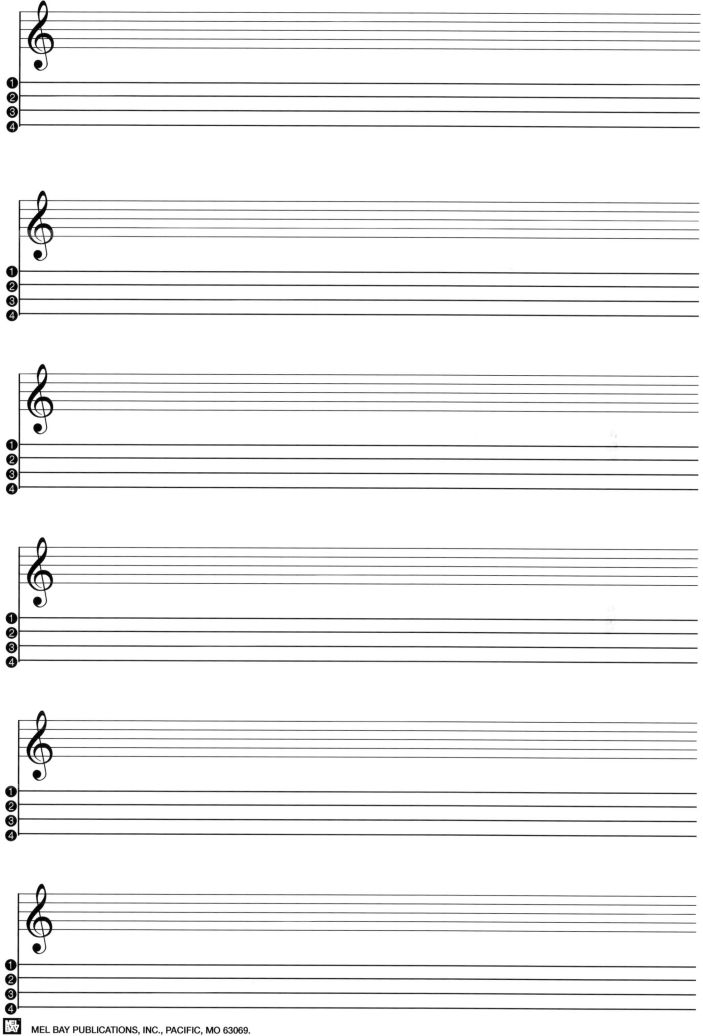

MEL BAY PUBLICATIONS, INC., PACIFIC, MO 63069.

MEL BAY PUBLICATIONS, INC., PACIFIC, MO 63069.

MEL BAY PUBLICATIONS, INC., PACIFIC, MO 63069.

MEL BAY PUBLICATIONS, INC., PACIFIC, MO 63069.

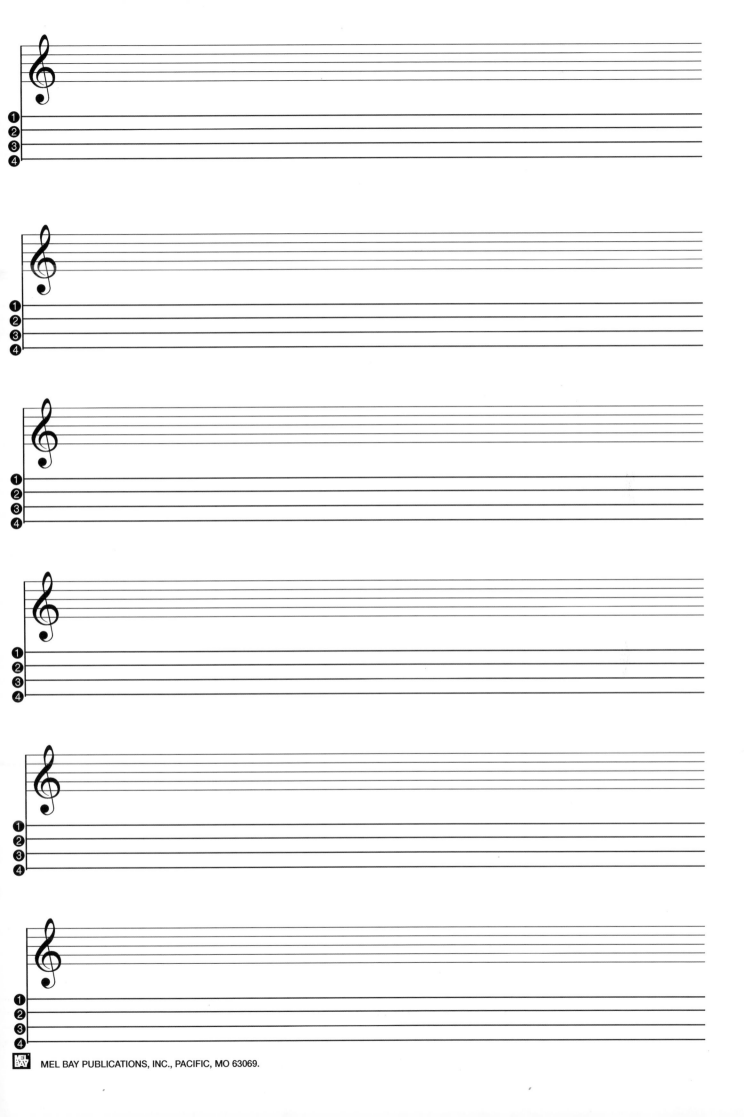

MEL BAY PUBLICATIONS, INC., PACIFIC, MO 63069.

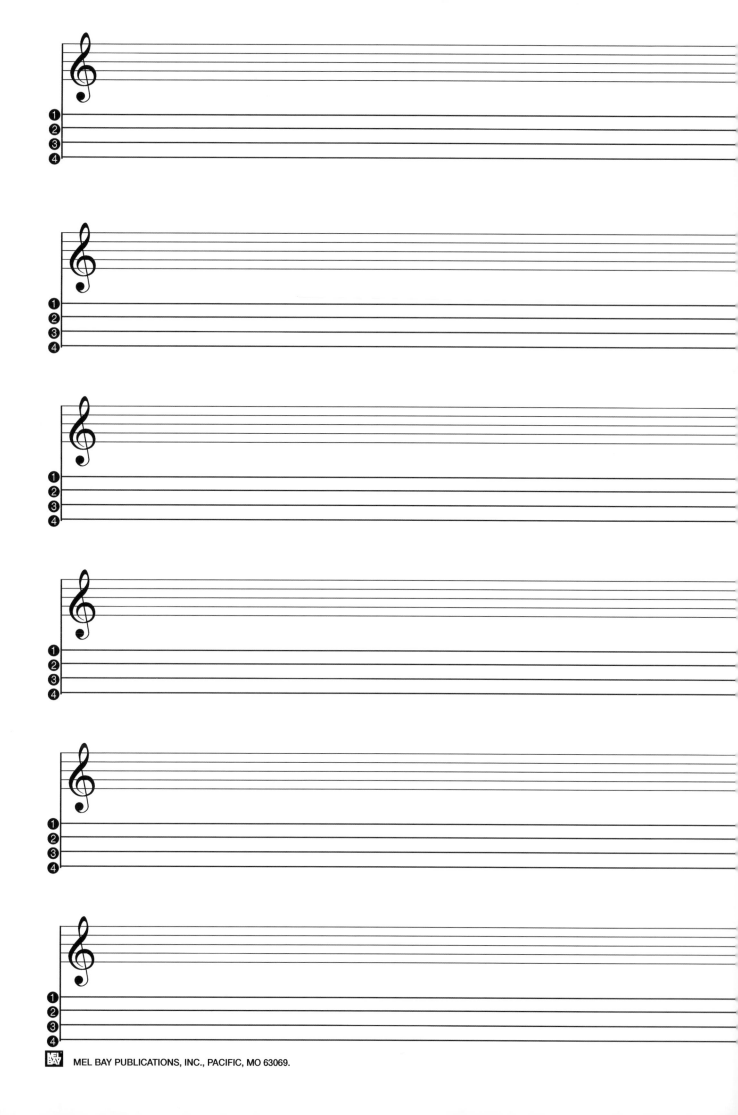

MEL BAY PUBLICATIONS, INC., PACIFIC, MO 63069.

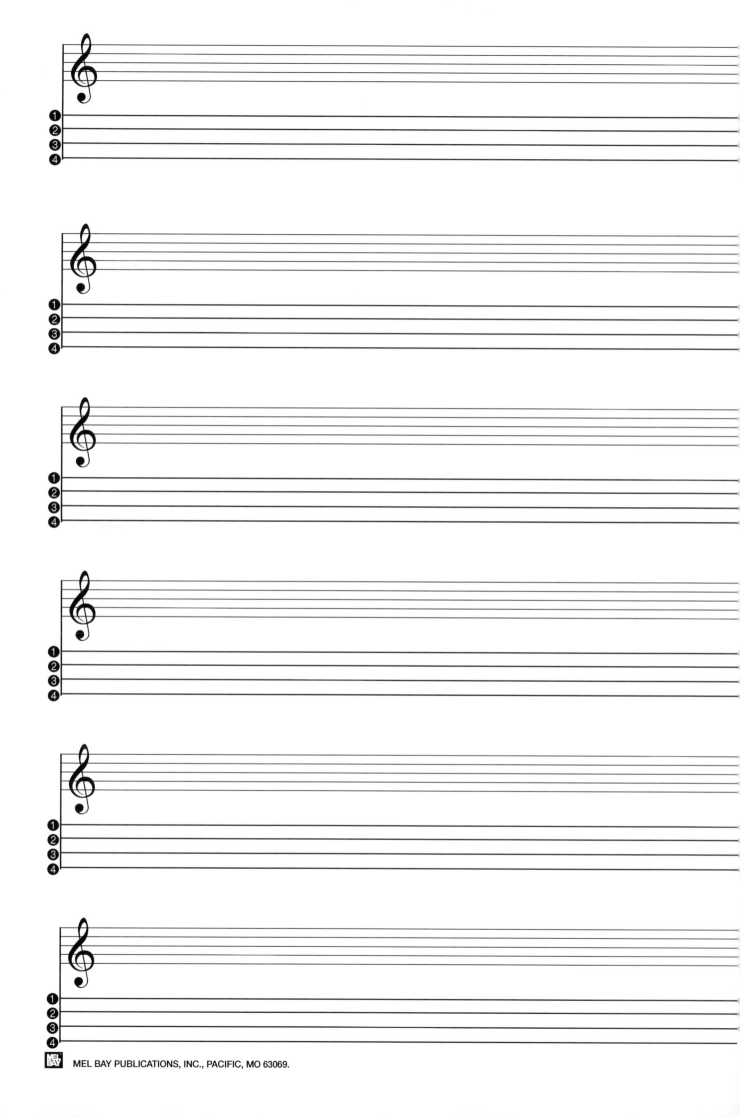

MEL BAY PUBLICATIONS, INC., PACIFIC, MO 63069.

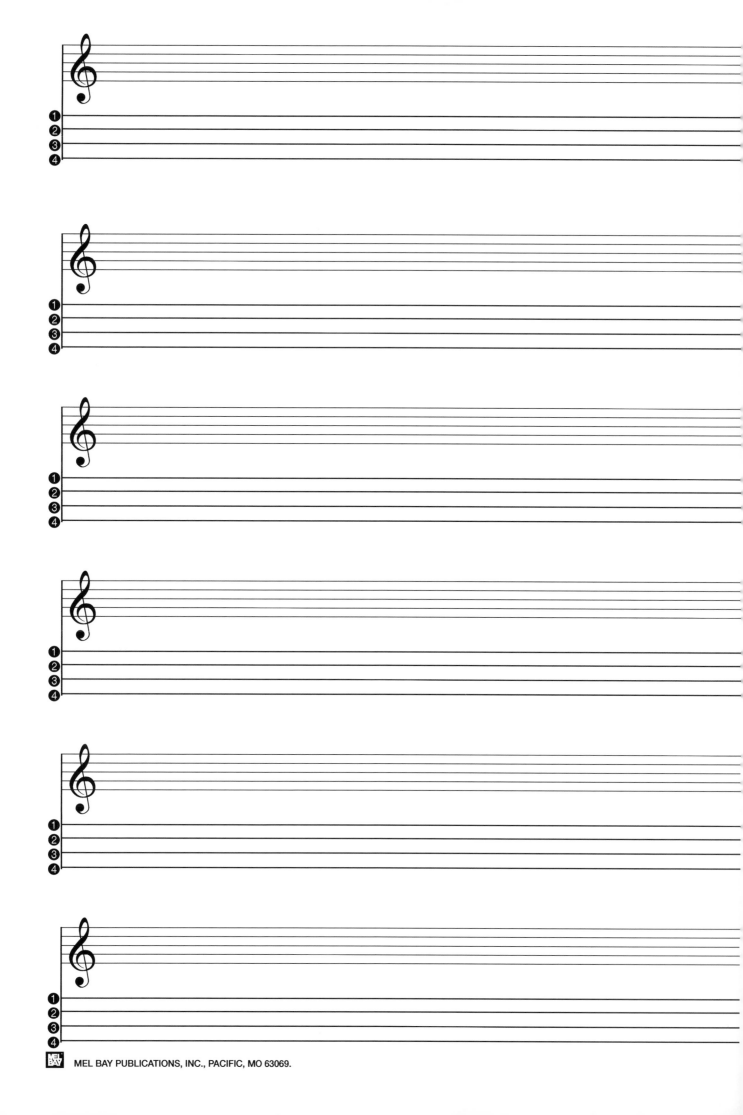

MEL BAY PUBLICATIONS, INC., PACIFIC, MO 63069.

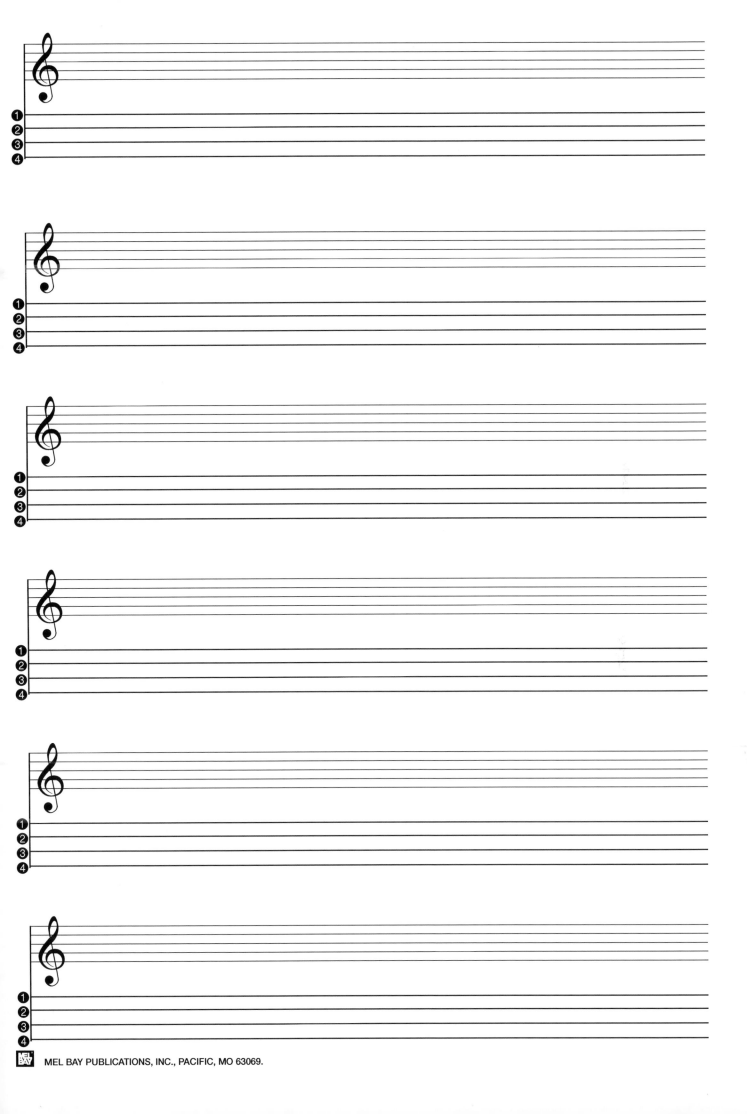

MEL BAY PUBLICATIONS, INC., PACIFIC, MO 63069.

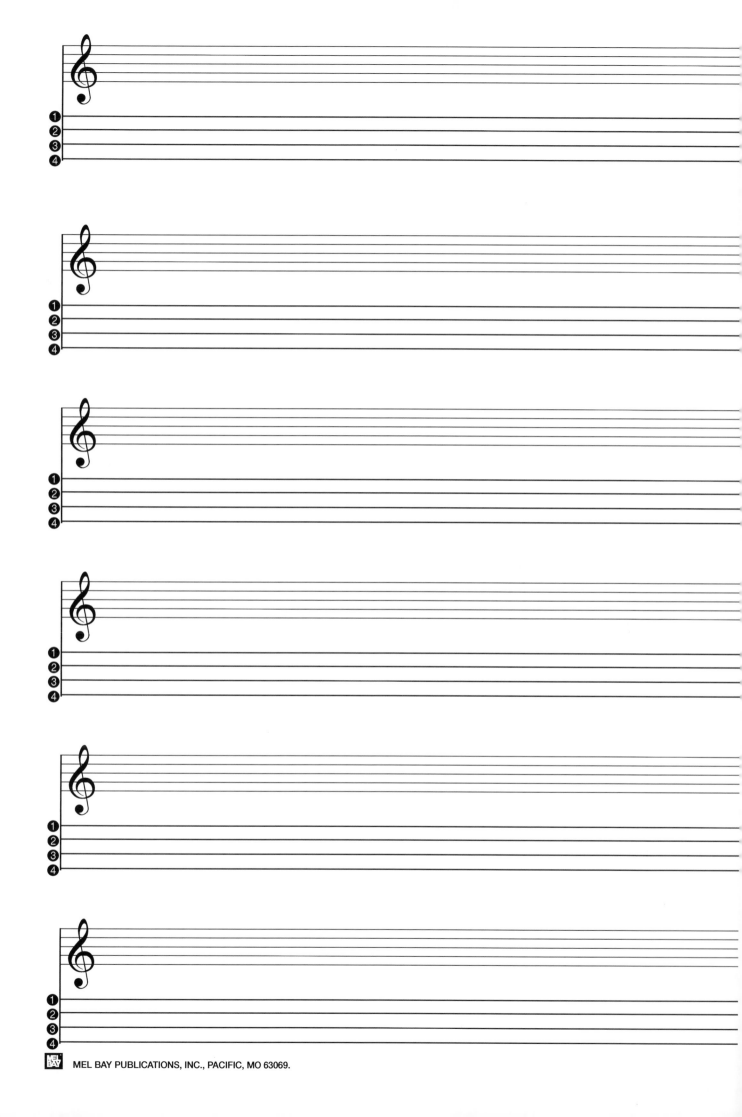

MEL BAY PUBLICATIONS, INC., PACIFIC, MO 63069.

MEL BAY PUBLICATIONS, INC., PACIFIC, MO 63069.

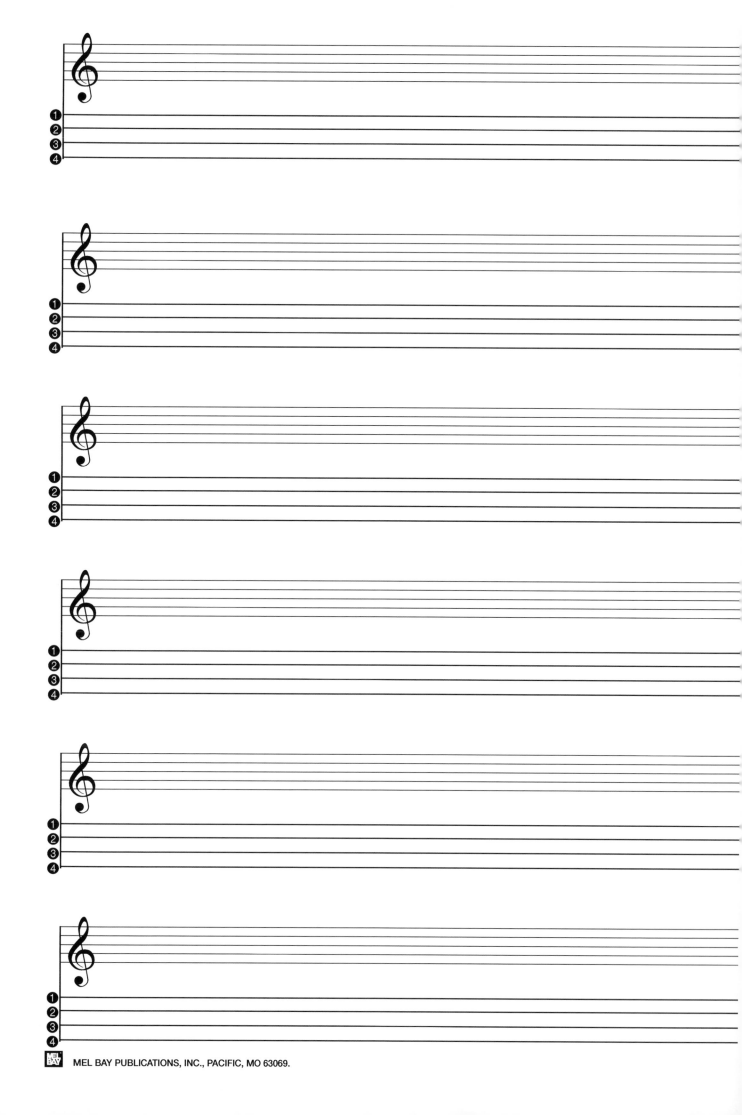

MEL BAY PUBLICATIONS, INC., PACIFIC, MO 63069.

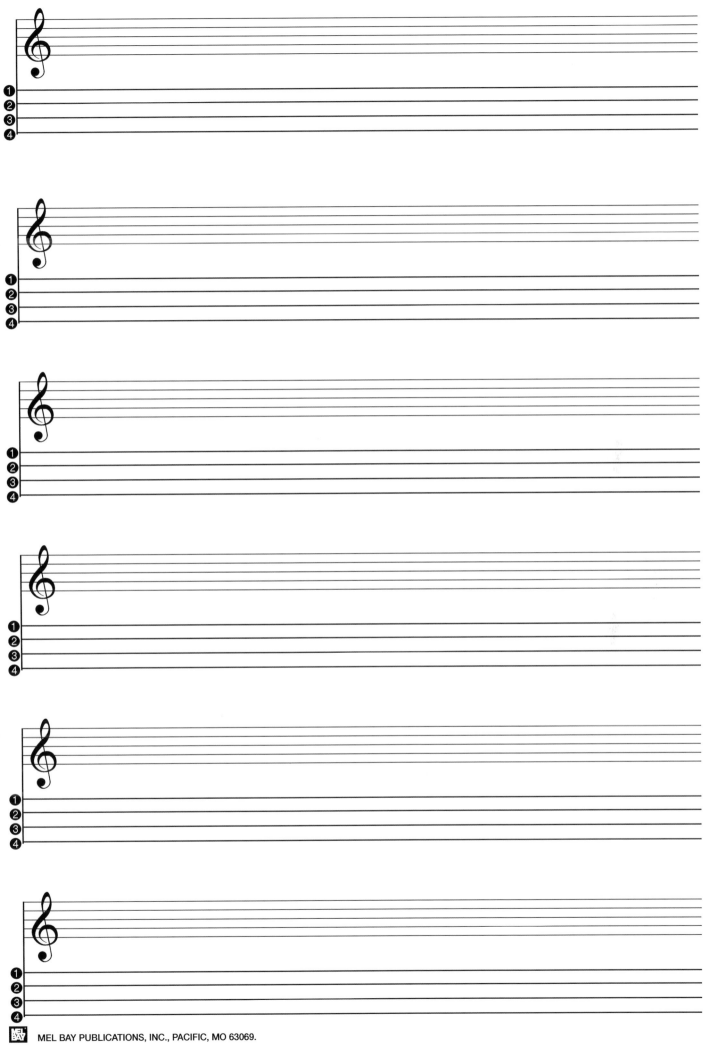

MEL BAY PUBLICATIONS, INC., PACIFIC, MO 63069.

MEL BAY PUBLICATIONS, INC., PACIFIC, MO 63069.

MEL BAY PUBLICATIONS, INC., PACIFIC, MO 63069.

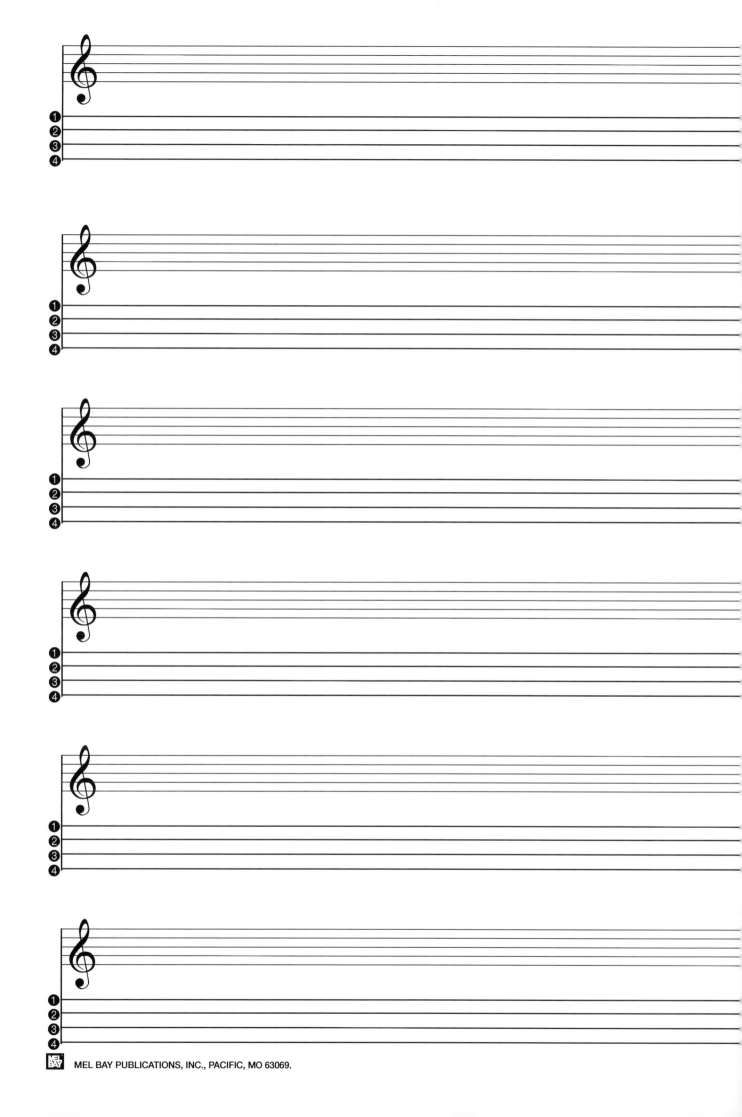

MEL BAY PUBLICATIONS, INC., PACIFIC, MO 63069.